I0448433

February 2013

DEFENSE HEALTH

Actions Needed to Help Ensure Combat Casualty Care Research Achieves Goals

Accountability ★ Integrity ★ Reliability

GAO-13-209

Highlights of GAO-13-209, a report to congressional committees

DEFENSE HEALTH

Actions Needed to Help Ensure Combat Casualty Care Research Achieves Goals

Why GAO Did This Study

DOD estimates that about 24 percent of servicemembers who die in combat could have survived if improved and more timely medical care could be made available. Because multiple DOD organizations conduct research to develop medical products and processes to improve combat casualty care, it is critical that these organizations coordinate their work. It is also important that agencies monitor and assess their performance to help achieve organizational goals, which for DOD include addressing gaps in its capability to provide combat casualty care. The National Defense Authorization Act for Fiscal Year 2012 directed GAO to review DOD's combat casualty care research and development programs. This report assesses whether DOD (1) uses a coordinated approach to plan this research; and (2) monitors and assesses this research to determine the extent to which it fills capability gaps and achieves other goals. GAO reviewed DOD's policies and documentation; interviewed officials from DOD and other federal agencies; and analyzed metrics DOD used to gauge the progress of its research.

What GAO Recommends

GAO recommends that DOD (1) communicate the importance of early coordination among DOD's nonmedical organizations and (2) develop and implement a plan to determine the extent to which research fills gaps and achieves other goals. DOD concurred with these recommendations.

View GAO-13-209. For more information, contact Linda T. Kohn (202) 512-7114 or kohnl@gao.gov, or Brenda S. Farrell, (202) 512-3604 or farrellb@gao.gov.

What GAO Found

The biomedical research organizations of the Department of Defense (DOD) use a coordinated approach to plan combat casualty care research and development, but not all of DOD's nonmedical research organizations share information early in the research process. GAO has previously reported that federal agencies can enhance and sustain collaboration of efforts by using key practices, such as agreeing on roles and responsibilities and establishing the means to operate across organizational boundaries. In 2010, DOD established a planning committee to coordinate the efforts of organizations conducting combat casualty care research. The committee developed a draft charter in 2010 identifying members respective roles and responsibilities. DOD issued the final charter in early January 2013, while GAO was conducting its review. DOD also facilitated operation across organizational boundaries by colocating most of the organizations conducting combat casualty care research. However, DOD organizations that typically do not conduct biomedical research, such as the Army Research Laboratory, are not involved in DOD's efforts to coordinate this research. When these organizations conduct research relevant to combat casualty care they do not always share information with appropriate officials early in the research process, as they are not aware of the need to coordinate early and may not fully understand medical research requirements. As a result, some researchers have had to repeat some work to adhere to these requirements. DOD has also taken steps to coordinate with other federal agencies that are involved in this research.

The Office of the Assistant Secretary of Defense for Health Affairs (Health Affairs) and the Army Medical Research and Materiel Command (MRMC) assess the progress of combat casualty care research and development projects, but they have not assessed the extent to which this research fills gaps in DOD's capability to provide this care or achieves other DOD goals. Federal internal control standards state that agencies should assess their performance to ensure they meet the agency's objectives. Health Affairs and Army MRMC—the two organizations that fund most combat casualty care research and development—monitor research projects to determine whether to continue funding, make necessary corrections, or terminate these projects. However, in 2008 DOD identified gaps in its capability to provide combat casualty care, and although Health Affairs and Army MRMC have completed 44 research projects since then designed to address these gaps, they have not assessed whether the results of this research fill the gaps identified in 2008. In addition, Health Affairs and Army MRMC established other goals for this research portfolio to improve combat casualty care. For example, in 2010, Health Affairs set goals to improve DOD's ability to control bleeding. However, neither organization has developed an assessment that comprehensively identifies each of the goals for the portfolio and includes information about the extent to which each goal has been met. Health Affairs and Army MRMC officials stated that they intend to complete a strategic roadmap for the portfolio, but GAO was unable to determine if the roadmap will include a plan for a comprehensive assessment of this portfolio. Without such a plan for a comprehensive assessment, these organizations cannot be sure the research they are conducting is producing results that most effectively improve combat casualty care to save lives on the battlefield.

_____ United States Government Accountability Office

Contents

Abbreviations

DARPA	Defense Advanced Research Projects Agency
DOD	Department of Defense
FDA	Food and Drug Administration
Health Affairs	Office of the Assistant Secretary of Defense for Health Affairs
HHS	Department of Health and Human Services
JPC-6	Joint Program Committee for Combat Casualty Care
MRMC	Army Medical Research and Materiel Command
NIH	National Institutes of Health
VA	Department of Veterans Affairs

United States Government Accountability Office
Washington, DC 20548

February 13, 2013

Congressional Committees

The Department of Defense (DOD) estimates that approximately 24 percent of all servicemembers who die in combat could have survived if improved and more timely medical care could be made available in the combat setting. To reduce the combat mortality rate as well as the impact of the disabling medical conditions that servicemembers suffer as a result of combat wounds, multiple DOD organizations conduct medical research to develop medical devices, pharmaceuticals, and new methods or processes that are designed to improve combat casualty care.[1] Using the results of this research, DOD intends to fill gaps that it identified in its capability to provide combat casualty care, such as its ability to control bleeding.[2] The Office of the Assistant Secretary of Defense for Health Affairs (Health Affairs), the military departments, and the Defense Advanced Research Projects Agency (DARPA) are responsible for this research, with funding of over $537 million in fiscal year 2010, $272 million in 2011, and $321 million in 2012. Because multiple organizations plan this research and development, it is important that they coordinate their actions to maximize their effectiveness in conducting the research, applying its findings, and producing results that ultimately save lives on the battlefield. It is also important that agencies monitor and assess their performance to help address organizational goals. For DOD, organizational goals include filling gaps in its capability to provide combat casualty care, such as improving DOD's ability to control bleeding, which is the primary cause of potentially survivable deaths on the battlefield. Such monitoring and assessment, as part of a system of effectively designed and implemented internal controls, provide reasonable assurance that an agency's operations are effective and efficient.[3]

---

[1] DOD officials define combat casualty care as the medical care provided to servicemembers from the time when they are wounded in combat through their hospitalization at a facility out of the combat theater, including evacuation and surgery.

[2] DOD, *Guidance for the Development of the Force FY2010–2015, Program and Budget Assessment A4.16, Medical Research and Development Investments* (June 2008).

[3] GAO, *Standards for Internal Control in the Federal Government*, GAO/AIMD-00-21.3.1 (Washington, D.C.: November 1999).

GAO-13-209 Defense Health

The National Defense Authorization Act for Fiscal Year 2012[4] directed GAO to review DOD's medical research and development programs designed to improve combat casualty care. The act requires GAO to evaluate aspects of DOD's combat casualty care research programs, including the extent to which DOD organizations coordinate their efforts to plan this research. In response to the act, this report addresses the extent to which DOD (1) uses a coordinated approach to plan for combat casualty care research and development and (2) monitors and assesses whether combat casualty care research and development fill capability gaps or achieve other goals.

To determine the extent to which DOD uses a coordinated approach to plan for combat casualty care research and development, we reviewed DOD's policies and documentation on coordinating research, and we analyzed various pertinent documents, including DOD summaries of the portfolio of ongoing research designed to improve combat casualty care. We also interviewed knowledgeable officials from various DOD organizations involved in planning this research and from other relevant federal agencies, including the Food and Drug Administration (FDA), the National Institutes of Health (NIH), and the Department of Veterans Affairs (VA). The DOD officials we interviewed include those from Health Affairs, which is organizationally aligned under the Under Secretary of Defense for Personnel and Readiness; the Assistant Secretary of Defense for Research and Engineering, which is organizationally aligned under the Under Secretary of Defense for Acquisition, Technology and Logistics; the Army Medical Research and Materiel Command (MRMC); the Office of Naval Research; the Naval Medical Research Center; the Air Force Medical Support Agency; and DARPA. Furthermore, we analyzed DOD's efforts to coordinate combat casualty care research and development by comparing those efforts to key collaboration practices that we previously reported, such as agreeing on roles and responsibilities and establishing a means to operate across organizational boundaries. We define both "collaboration" and "coordination" as any joint activity by two or more organizations intended to produce more public value than could be produced when the organizations act alone.[5] To determine the extent to which DOD monitors and assesses whether

---

[4]Pub. L. No. 112-81, § 1076, 125 Stat. 1298, 1595-1596 (2011).

[5]GAO, *Results-Oriented Government: Practices That Can Help Enhance and Sustain Collaboration among Federal Agencies*, GAO-06-15 (Washington, D.C.: Oct. 21, 2005).

GAO-13-209 Defense Health

combat casualty care research and development fill capability gaps or achieve other goals, we obtained and analyzed data from Health Affairs, the military departments, and DARPA regarding metrics the department uses that gauge the progress and performance of its research projects. We also interviewed knowledgeable officials from a variety of DOD organizations, including the Army Institute for Surgical Research and the Naval Medical Research Center, about their monitoring efforts to apply findings from research. In addition, we reviewed the relevant internal control standards for the federal government, which address monitoring and assessing performance, and compared DOD's efforts to these standards.[6] We focused this portion of our analysis on Health Affairs and the Army because they are responsible for the majority of combat casualty care research in DOD, with over 82 percent of DOD's combat casualty care funding in 2012.

We conducted this performance audit from May 2012 to February 2013 in accordance with generally accepted government auditing standards. Those standards require that we plan and perform the audit to obtain sufficient, appropriate evidence to provide a reasonable basis for our findings and conclusions based on our audit objectives. We believe that the evidence obtained provides a reasonable basis for our findings and conclusions based on our audit objectives.

Background

Application of Combat Casualty Care Research Findings

DOD's combat casualty care researchers focus their efforts on the major causes of injury and death on the battlefield, and on improving medical care in specific battlefield conditions. For example, DOD estimates that approximately 84 percent of potentially survivable battlefield deaths are caused by bleeding. Therefore, DOD focuses a significant amount of its research on ways to control bleeding on the battlefield. Other areas on which DOD researchers focus include extremity trauma, diagnosis and treatment of traumatic brain injury, and ways to improve the care provided to casualties prior to and during evacuation to a hospital.

---

[6]GAO/AIMD-00-21.3.1.

In order to improve medical care in these areas, DOD researchers use various means to apply findings from combat casualty care research to develop drugs or medical devices. For example, DOD researchers convene multidisciplinary teams to decide whether a research project is ready and feasible to support development of a drug or medical device, according to DOD officials. These teams consist of researchers and other DOD personnel who are involved in acquiring and maintaining drugs and medical devices. At multiple meetings, the teams make decisions on whether to allow the project to proceed. In addition, DOD researchers work with the FDA to understand and share general information about regulatory requirements for drugs and medical devices that DOD develops. DOD officials also told us that in some cases DOD researchers also share the results of DOD research with medical corporations, which develop these products.

In addition to developing drugs or medical devices, DOD researchers apply findings from combat casualty care research by disseminating information on medical practices. For example, the Army Institute for Surgical Research publishes clinical-practice guidelines that clinical subject-matter experts develop in response to needs identified while providing care to combat casualties. These guidelines are based on the best existing clinical evidence and experience, approved by senior DOD medical officials, and are available to all military medical practitioners. In addition, DOD researchers share new medical knowledge and best-practice information by publishing research results in medical journals and making presentations at conferences.

Combat Casualty Care Research Capability Gaps and Funding

In May 2008, then–Secretary of Defense Robert Gates publicly expressed his commitment to improving medical care and support for wounded servicemembers. In that same month, DOD completed a program assessment of its medical research and development investments, which became the basis for DOD's June 2008 *Guidance for the Development of the Force* report.[7] Among other matters, this assessment identified gaps in DOD's capabilities to protect the health of servicemembers, including health care provided to servicemembers who are wounded on the battlefield. For example, the 2008 report identified a gap in DOD's capability to diagnose, resuscitate, and stabilize casualties with survivable

---

[7]DOD, *Guidance for the Development of the Force FY2010–2015.*

wounds. DOD used the capability gaps identified in the 2008 report as the justification for funding requests that DOD subsequently made for medical research and development, including for research to address gaps in DOD's capability to provide combat casualty care. This assessment also concluded that a consolidated medical research and development budget structure with a centralized planning, programming, and budget authority and with centralized management would provide the most efficient and effective process and governance for DOD's medical research and development investment.[8]

To address the gaps in its capability to provide combat casualty care, DOD has increased this research funding overall, as shown in figure 1.

Figure 1: DOD Combat Casualty Care Research and Development Funding from Fiscal Year 2005 through Fiscal Year 2012

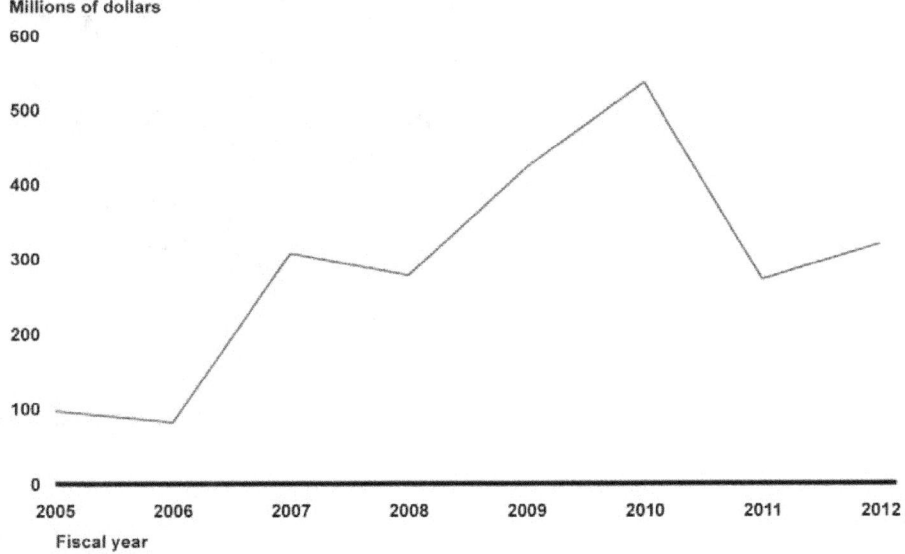

Source: GAO analysis of DOD information.

---

[8]GAO, *Defense Health Care: Applying Key Management Practices Should Help Achieve Efficiencies within the Military Heath System*, GAO-12-224 (Washington, D.C.: Apr. 12, 2012).

In fiscal year 2010, DOD's funding for combat casualty care research increased to $537 million, and 2 years later it fell to $321 million. Health Affairs and the Army, with 82 percent of the funding in fiscal year 2012, were responsible for the majority of this research (see fig. 2). The Navy, the Air Force, and DARPA were responsible for the remainder.

Figure 2: Percent of Fiscal Year 2012 Combat Casualty Care Research and Development Funding by Organization

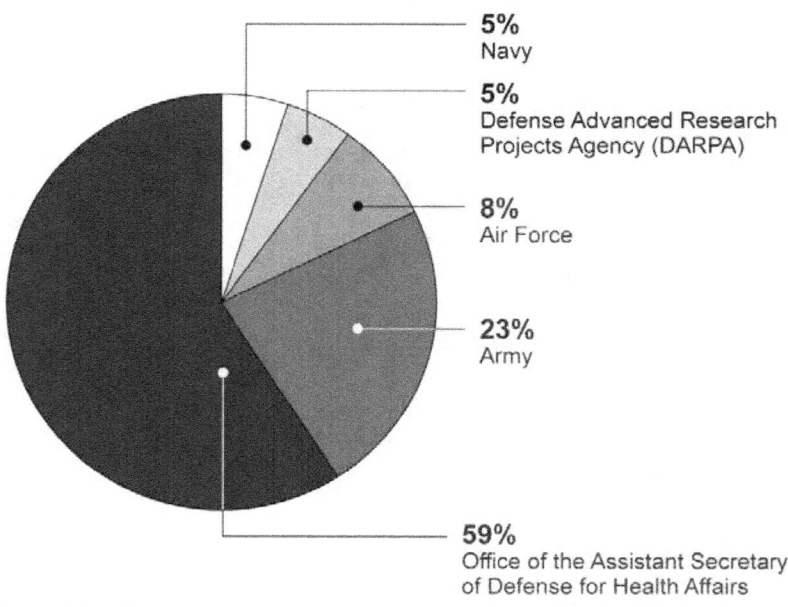

5%
Navy

5%
Defense Advanced Research Projects Agency (DARPA)

8%
Air Force

23%
Army

59%
Office of the Assistant Secretary of Defense for Health Affairs

Source: GAO analysis of DOD information.

Note: Funding for combat casualty care research and development totaled $321 million in fiscal year 2012. This amount does not include funding for other DOD organizations that do not typically conduct combat casualty care research but sometimes conduct research that is related to combat casualty care.

Multiple DOD Organizations Oversee and Plan Research and Development

Multiple officials and organizations oversee DOD's combat casualty care research and development. The Assistant Secretary of Defense for Research and Engineering—who reports to the Under Secretary of Defense for Acquisition, Technology and Logistics—is responsible for promoting coordination of all research and engineering within DOD, including health-related research such as combat casualty care research. In addition, the Assistant Secretary of Defense for Health Affairs serves as the principal advisor to the Under Secretary of Defense for Personnel and Readiness on a variety of health issues, including medical research, which includes research to improve combat casualty care. The Assistant Secretary of Defense for Research and Engineering and the Assistant Secretary of Defense for Health Affairs cochair the Armed Services Biomedical Research and Evaluation Management committee. This committee's charter states that it was established to facilitate coordination and prevent unnecessary duplication of effort within DOD's biomedical research and development program. Joint Technology Coordinating Groups[9] support the committee in specific research areas, including combat casualty care. Joint Technology Coordinating Groups are responsible for coordinating plans for research in their areas and for submitting recommendations on the distribution of responsibility for program execution and resources. (See fig. 3 for organizations that oversee combat casualty care research and development.)

Figure 3: Organizations That Oversee Combat Casualty Care Research and Development

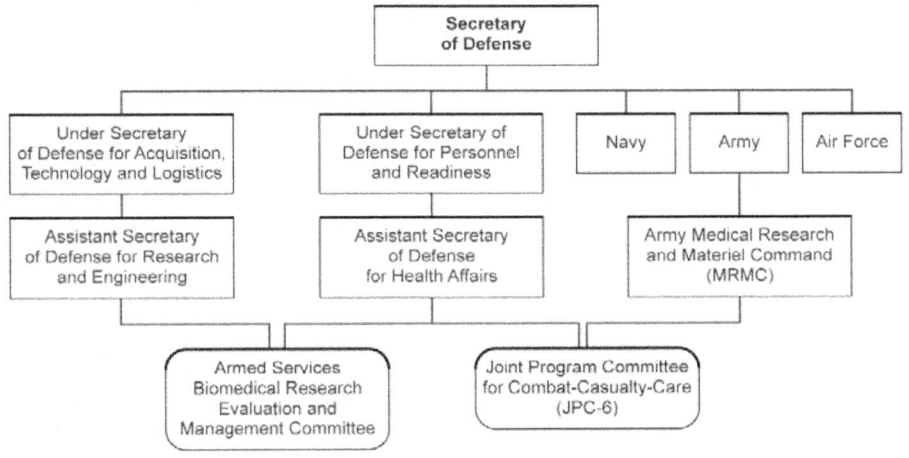

Source: GAO analysis of DOD information.

Note: The JPC-6 includes representatives from each military service (Army, Navy, Air Force, and Marine Corps) and is chartered by Army Medical Research and Materiel Command (MRMC).

---

[9]Joint Technology Coordinating Groups are composed of a single member from each of the Army, Navy, and Air Force.

GAO-13-209 Defense Health

With regard to planning, there are multiple DOD organizations specifically devoted to biomedical research, and these organizations plan research and development designed to improve the medical care provided to injured servicemembers. They include the Army MRMC, the Office of Naval Research, the Naval Medical Research Center, the Air Force Office of Scientific Research, the Air Force Medical Support Agency, and DARPA. In March 2011, Health Affairs signed an interagency support agreement with the Army MRMC to take advantage of existing Army MRMC staff and infrastructure. Under the agreement, the Army MRMC manages certain Health Affairs funds for medical research and development. To help manage these funds, the Army MRMC established Joint Program Committees for the major areas of medical research that DOD conducts, including combat casualty care, which is managed by the Joint Program Committee for Combat Casualty Care (JPC-6). The JPC-6 includes representatives from the DOD biomedical research organizations within each military department, including the Marine Corps, as well as from DARPA, NIH, VA, and other DOD organizations that use the results of combat casualty care research—such as DOD's Special Operations Command. These organizations coordinate to prioritize how to spend the Health Affairs funding for combat casualty care research.

Other DOD research organizations also conduct research that is at times related to combat casualty care. Typically these research organizations do not plan or conduct biomedical research, but sometimes they identify ways that applications of their research could improve combat casualty care. These organizations include the Army Research Laboratory and the Naval Postgraduate School.

DOD Uses a Coordinated Approach to Plan Its Combat Casualty Care Research and Development, but Not All of Its Organizations Share Information Early

DOD's biomedical research organizations use a coordinated approach to plan for combat casualty care research and development in a manner that is consistent with key collaboration practices. Further, DOD research organizations do not always share information early in the research process. DOD has also taken steps to coordinate with other federal agencies that are involved in combat casualty care research.

DOD's Combat Casualty Care Research Planning Is Consistent with Key Collaboration Practices

DOD's biomedical research organizations coordinate combat casualty care research and development planning in a manner that is consistent with key collaboration practices identified in prior GAO work to enhance and sustain coordination.[10] These key practices include agreeing on roles and responsibilities and establishing a means to operate across organizational boundaries.

Agreement on Roles and Responsibilities

DOD's biomedical research organizations responsible for combat casualty care research and development have agreed on their roles and responsibilities, including establishing a key leadership position responsible for combat casualty care research. As we have previously reported, agreement on roles and responsibilities among coordinating organizations is important because it enables each organization to stay informed about the others' individual and joint efforts, and it facilitates decision making.

DOD's biomedical research organizations have agreed on the roles and responsibilities for the organizations involved in planning, overseeing, and executing this type of research. First, Health Affairs and the Army MRMC—the two organizations that fund most combat casualty care research and development—have outlined their roles in an Interagency Support Agreement, which designates the Army MRMC as the organization responsible for managing the day-to-day use of Health Affairs funding for medical research, including research to improve combat casualty care. Second, the JPC-6 developed a draft charter in 2010 that explains the roles and responsibilities for all of the JPC-6 member organizations, including the non-DOD organizations, such as VA and NIH. The draft charter was finalized in early January 2013, while we were conducting our review.[11] Health Affairs and Army MRMC officials told us that the JPC-6 began using the charter in 2010, but that they delayed finalizing it in part because they wanted to have the opportunity to incorporate lessons learned during the operation of the committee during its first 2 years. The charter states that JPC-6 members represent the interests of their member organizations as well as provide subject-matter expertise and advice to the JPC-6 chair on requirements, program

---

[10]GAO-06-15.

[11]DOD, *US Army Medical Research and Materiel Command Joint Program Committee-6 Charter for the Combat Casualty Care JPC*, (Jan. 2, 2013).

management, transition planning, and planning and programming for future investments.

In addition to establishing a JPC-6 charter, Health Affairs and Army MRMC have established a key leadership position responsible for combat casualty care research by having one official serve simultaneously in three complementary roles: JPC-6 chair, Director of the Army Combat Casualty Care Research Program, and chair of the Joint Technology Coordinating Group for Combat Casualty Care. As noted in the JPC-6 charter, the group's chair is responsible for making recommendations to Health Affairs for planning, programming, budgeting, and executing research and development to improve medical care provided to combat casualties, and the chair is to make these recommendations with the advice and support of the JPC-6 members. Because the DOD official serving as JPC-6 chair also serves as Director of the Army Combat Casualty Care Research Program and chair of the Joint Technology Coordinating Group for Combat Casualty Care, this official oversees the majority of this research in DOD. From fiscal years 2008 through 2011, this official oversaw approximately 600 research projects, constituting over 80 percent of DOD's funding for combat casualty care research. Health Affairs and Army MRMC officials told us they expect that one official will lead all three organizations in the future.

Means to Operate across Organizational Boundaries

DOD's biomedical research organizations responsible for combat casualty care research and development have established mechanisms to facilitate working across organizational boundaries—a step that, as we have previously reported, helps to enhance and sustain coordination.[12] For example, DOD located nearly all of the DOD biomedical research organizations that conduct combat casualty care research at the Joint Center of Excellence for Battlefield Health and Trauma Research at Fort Sam Houston, Texas.[13] The center includes the U.S. Army Institute for Surgical Research and other principal DOD biomedical research organizations that conduct combat casualty care research, such as the combat casualty care research functions from the Naval Medical Research Center and from Walter Reed Army Institute of Research. DOD

---

[12]GAO-06-15.

[13]DOD established this center in response to a recommendation in the 2005 Base Realignment and Closure Report. DOD, *2005 Base Closure and Realignment Report*, vol. X (Washington, D.C.: May 9, 2005).

officials told us that being located in the same place is useful in enabling them to know what other DOD organizations are doing with their related research and development. Another example of a mechanism to facilitate working across organizational boundaries is the Military Health System Research Symposium, an annual conference that provides DOD researchers the opportunity to discuss and address multiple medical research topics, including combat casualty care, with researchers from other federal agencies, academia, and private industry. DOD officials told us that these annual conferences have led to interagency collaboration on research and development for combat casualty care.

Other DOD Research Organizations Do Not Always Coordinate Early in the Research Process, Which Can Result in Inefficiencies

DOD organizations that typically do not conduct biomedical research are generally not involved in DOD's efforts to coordinate combat casualty care research. When these nonmedical research organizations conduct research relevant to combat casualty care, they do not always share relevant information with appropriate officials early in the research process. We have previously reported that organizations involved in similar missions should coordinate and share relevant information early to avoid unnecessary duplication of work.[14]

The JPC-6 chair, who is the lead official responsible for coordinating combat casualty care research, told us that he periodically has identified cases in which researchers began conducting research relevant to combat casualty care, but did not coordinate with him early in the process. He stated that in these cases, the research typically had been underway for a period of 1 to 5 years before he learned about it. He stated that he coordinates with nonmedical research organizations when he becomes aware of research relevant to combat casualty care. However, he stated that he has not always been aware of relevant research, and that there may be similar ongoing research projects about

---

[14]GAO, *Interagency Collaboration: Key Issues for Congressional Oversight of National Security Strategies, Organizations, Workforce, and Information Sharing*, GAO-09-904SP (Washington, D.C.: Sept. 25, 2009) and *Managing for Results: Using the Results Act to Address Mission Fragmentation and Program Overlap*, GAO/AIMD-97-146 (Washington, D.C.: Aug. 29, 1997). For more information on fragmentation, overlap, and duplication in federal programs see GAO, *2012 Annual Report: Opportunities to Reduce Potential Duplication in Government Programs, Save Tax Dollars, and Enhance Revenue*, GAO-11-318SP (Washington, D.C.: Mar. 1, 2011) and *Opportunities to Reduce Duplication, Overlap and Fragmentation, Achieve Savings, and Enhance Revenue*, GAO-12-342SP (Washington, D.C.: Feb. 28, 2012).

GAO-13-209 Defense Health

which he is currently unaware. For example, the Army Research Laboratory, which typically conducts research in the physical, engineering, and environmental sciences, started developing a product in 2006 that had the potential to control the bleeding of wounded soldiers—the leading cause of preventable deaths on the battlefield—but did not inform the JPC-6 chair of this research until 2 years later. In addition, multiple DOD officials—including the JPC-6 chair and other officials responsible for health research—stated that other DOD research organizations, such as the Naval Postgraduate School, the Defense Threat Reduction Agency, and the Joint Improvised Explosive Device Defeat Organization, have conducted research related to combat casualty care in the past and have not always coordinated or shared information early in the research process.

The JPC-6 chair also stated that some DOD researchers do not share information with him early in the research process because they are not aware of the need to coordinate early and may not fully understand medical research requirements, such as those that are necessary to support FDA processes for approval of new drugs and medical devices. He also stated that a lack of awareness and understanding can result in researchers duplicating each other's work. As discussed above, Army Research Laboratory researchers did not inform the JPC-6 chair of their work for 2 years, and as a result they learned that some of their initial testing did not fully adhere to medical testing protocols associated with wounds and wound severity. Subsequently, the researchers had to redo some steps in their research. An Army Research Laboratory official responsible for the project told us that they could have avoided the inefficiency of duplicating these steps if they had shared information with the JPC-6 chair at an earlier point. The JPC-6 chair stated that, since this occurrence, the Army Research Laboratory and Army MRMC now coordinate with one another regularly to identify Army Research Laboratory projects with potential implications for combat casualty care.

DOD Takes Steps to Coordinate with the FDA and Federal Agencies That Conduct Research Related to Combat Casualty Care

DOD coordinates medical research information with other federal agencies, including FDA, NIH, and VA. DOD coordinates with FDA with regard to drugs and medical devices it develops because FDA is responsible for overseeing the safety and effectiveness of these products—including those that are developed through DOD's combat casualty care research—and DOD must obtain FDA's regulatory review and approval or clearance to field medical products. FDA officials stated that they regularly meet with the commanding general of the Army MRMC to review DOD's medical research priorities and to share general information about regulatory requirements. FDA officials also provide product-specific advice to DOD regarding regulatory requirements by meeting with DOD researchers throughout the development process. This coordination is consistent with FDA's efforts, noted in previous GAO reports, to address concerns from industry and advocacy groups, including those related to the timeliness of the review process and the need to improve communication between FDA and stakeholders throughout the development process.[15] DOD officials told us that FDA regulators were very responsive to their regulatory questions and concerns, and they reported that sometimes this communication helped to expedite the development process.

Likewise, it is important for DOD, NIH, and VA to coordinate with each other because all of these agencies conduct research that is directly related to combat casualty care research. DOD, NIH, and VA conduct joint program reviews, prepare joint strategic documents, complete joint research projects, and attend joint symposiums and conferences to share their research. Our prior work identified some issues concerning the ability of DOD, NIH, and VA to readily access comprehensive medical research information funded by the other agencies.[16] We found that the three agencies could improve their ability to efficiently identify potential duplication if they improved access to each others' comprehensive electronic information on funded health research. DOD officials recently stated that DOD and the other two agencies are working together to address these concerns. Specifically, NIH has provided a DOD official with access to an NIH database that contains information about funded health research projects, and it has also provided training and support so that the DOD official can search the database for potential duplicated research. If this effort is successful, DOD plans to identify additional medical research officials who will be granted access to NIH's health research database. Because VA's medical research information resides

---

[15]GAO, *Prescription Drugs: FDA Has Met Most Performance Goals for Reviewing Applications*, GAO-12-500 (Washington, D.C.: Mar. 30, 2012) and *Medical Devices: FDA Has Met Most Performance Goals but Device Reviews Are Taking Longer*, GAO-12-418 (Washington, D.C.: Feb. 29, 2012).

[16]GAO-12-342SP.

in this database, DOD will also be able to identify VA research that is directly related to DOD's combat casualty care research.[17]

DOD Monitors the Progress of Combat Casualty Care Research Projects, but Not Whether the Research Fills Gaps or Achieves Other Goals

Health Affairs and Army MRMC monitor and assess the progress of combat casualty care research and development projects, but they have not assessed the extent to which this research fills gaps in DOD's capability to provide combat casualty care or achieves other goals for this research, including those related to improving DOD's ability to control bleeding, which is the primary cause of death on the battlefield. Internal control standards for the federal government state that agencies should monitor and assess their performance over time to help ensure that they meet the agency's missions, goals, and objectives.[18] Using performance information such as performance metrics can aid agencies with monitoring results, developing approaches to improve results, and helping determine progress in meeting the goals of programs or operations.

Health Affairs and Army MRMC monitor and assess the progress of combat casualty care research and development projects. For example, Health Affairs and Army MRMC monitor and assess cost, schedule, and performance metrics for individual research projects to determine whether to continue funding, make necessary corrections to, or terminate these projects. Senior leadership in these organizations reviews projects annually to determine whether they are meeting established cost, schedule, and performance baselines. In addition, these leaders assess technology readiness levels—which are measurements of maturity level—to determine whether findings from a research project are sufficiently mature to move to the next phase of development. Health Affairs and Army MRMC also monitor and assess some aspects of the progress of the overall combat casualty care research portfolio, such as the number of projects completed, ongoing, or canceled, as well as the number of products available to users in the field. These organizations have applied findings from combat casualty care research to field five such products between fiscal years 2008 and 2011. For example, Health Affairs and Army MRMC officials told us that DOD fielded a combat gauze

---

[17]As noted in GAO-12-342SP, NIH also maintains a public database containing award data on NIH-funded health research, which DOD officials could search for potential duplicative research.

[18]GAO/AIMD-00-21.3.1.

product that was the result of combat casualty care research. This gauze includes a mineral to help form blood clots and is designed to stop severe bleeding in less than 4 minutes. Following the annual combat casualty care research portfolio review in September 2012, Health Affairs and Army MRMC reported that they plan to identify new performance metrics, such as data related to peer-reviewed publications and FDA approved drugs and medical devices that will provide additional information on the overall portfolio's progress.

However, Health Affairs and Army MRMC have not assessed the extent to which the results of combat casualty care research fill gaps in DOD's capability to provide care to combat casualties. As we discussed earlier, DOD identified a number of gaps in its capability to provide combat casualty care in the 2008 *Guidance for the Development of the Force* analysis and report.[19] Since 2008, Health Affairs and Army MRMC told us that they have completed about 44 combat casualty care research projects that are each designed to address one or more of these capability gaps. Health Affairs and Army MRMC officials told us that in 2010 they attempted to measure the extent to which the 2008 capability gaps had been filled on the basis of the research results. However, they abandoned that effort because, according to officials, in 2010 researchers had not completed a sufficient amount of research designed to fill the 2008 capability gaps. In addition, these officials indicated that the capability gaps were not specific, were not organized to correspond with DOD's research areas, and did not reflect the state of medical knowledge at the time. Health Affairs officials told us that they are currently revising these capability gaps and they expect to complete the revision in 2013. Following the Health Affairs revision, the Joint Staff—a group of senior military leaders in DOD—will then validate the capability gaps. Health Affairs and Army MRMC officials told us that they plan to assess whether the results of future research fill the revised capability gaps once the Joint Staff validates them.

In addition, Health Affairs and Army MRMC have not developed an assessment of the extent to which the results of combat casualty care research have achieved other goals for this research. Both Health Affairs and Army MRMC have established goals for the combat casualty care research portfolio including several related to improving DOD's ability to

---

[19]DOD, *Guidance for the Development of the Force FY2010–2015.*

control bleeding, which is the primary cause of death on the battlefield. For example, Health Affairs set a goal for DOD to improve its ability to control bleeding in areas of the human body where it is not feasible to apply a tourniquet, such as on internal organs or the groin. Health Affairs and Army MRMC officials told us that they periodically review and discuss progress toward these research goals for certain research topics. However, these officials have not developed an assessment that comprehensively identifies each of the goals for the portfolio and includes information about the extent to which each goal has been met. They acknowledged that more work is needed to do this. Following a review and analysis of the combat casualty care research portfolio in September 2012, Health Affairs and Army MRMC officials reported to us that they intended to complete an overarching strategic roadmap for the portfolio by March 2013. They told us that they expect the roadmap could include specific project timelines and goals, among other things. However, on the basis of the information provided by DOD officials, we were unable to determine if the plan will clearly delineate how Health Affairs and Army MRMC will assess the extent to which results from combat casualty care projects fill capability gaps and achieve other goals. Until Health Affairs and Army MRMC assess the results of DOD's research against revised capability gaps and other goals, DOD will not have reasonable assurance that the research it is conducting meets its needs.

Conclusions

Coordination among the various organizations that plan and conduct combat casualty care research and development is important to effectively produce medical solutions to save or improve the lives of injured servicemembers. DOD has taken important steps to agree on roles and responsibilities and to establish the means for coordination and collaboration across organizational boundaries. However, DOD's research organizations can only coordinate with each other when they become aware of relevant research. Without communicating to nonmedical research organizations about the importance of coordinating with the JPC-6 chair early in the research process, DOD research organizations may have to redo some steps of their research to address medical research requirements that they may not fully understand. Moreover, while DOD assesses the progress of combat casualty care research projects, it is also important that DOD monitor and assess the extent to which the results of its combat casualty care research fill the gaps in DOD's capability to provide combat casualty care and achieve other goals that it established for the research. However, without a plan for monitoring and assessment, DOD runs the risk that it may not be producing results that most effectively improve combat casualty care to save lives on the battlefield.

Recommendations for Executive Action

1. To ensure that nonmedical DOD research organizations coordinate with the Assistant Secretary of Defense for Health Affairs early in the research process to understand medical research requirements and avoid inefficiencies that may lead to duplicative work, we recommend that the Secretary of Defense direct the Under Secretary of Defense for Acquisition, Technology and Logistics to

   - communicate to DOD's nonmedical research organizations the importance of coordination with the JPC-6 chair on combat casualty care issues, and require this coordination early in the research process when these organizations conduct research with implications for combat casualty care.

2. To improve DOD's ability to assess the overall performance of its combat casualty care research portfolio, we recommend that the Secretary of Defense direct the Under Secretary of Defense for Personnel and Readiness to direct the Assistant Secretary of Defense for Health Affairs to

   - develop and implement a plan to assess the extent to which combat casualty care research and development fills gaps in DOD's capability to provide combat casualty care and achieves DOD's other goals for this portfolio of research.

Agency Comments and Our Evaluation

We provided a draft of this report to DOD, VA, and the Department of Health and Human Services (HHS), which includes FDA and NIH. In response, we received written comments from DOD and HHS, which are reprinted in appendixes I and II, respectively. VA did not comment on this report. DOD and HHS also provided technical comments that we have incorporated as appropriate.

Department of Defense

In its written comments, DOD concurred with the recommendations we made to the department and also described steps it had taken or planned to take in response to our recommendations. Specifically, DOD concurred with our first recommendation to communicate to nonmedical research organizations the importance of coordination with the JPC-6 chair and require this coordination early in the research process. DOD also concurred with our second recommendation to develop and implement a plan to assess the extent to which combat casualty care research addresses DOD's capability gaps and achieves its other goals. In its comments on our second recommendation, DOD stated that it planned to revise its process to better assess the extent to which each combat casualty care research project closes capability gaps. Moreover, when we sent our draft report to DOD for comment in December 2012, Health Affairs and Army MRMC had not yet finalized the JPC-6 charter. Therefore, we included a recommendation in our draft report that DOD issue the final charter. In early January 2013, after we sent the draft report to DOD, the commanding general of Army MRMC signed and issued the final JPC-6 charter. As a result, we did not include the recommendation to finalize the charter in our final report.

Department of Health and Human Services

In its written comments, HHS responded to a statement in the draft report that DOD, NIH, and VA could improve their ability to efficiently identify potentially duplicative research with improved access to each agency's electronic health research information, as noted in a 2012 GAO report.[20] HHS stated that DOD has access, to varying degrees, to NIH and VA medical research information. Consistent with our 2012 report, HHS stated that NIH and VA need access to DOD medical research information to reduce the risk of potentially duplicative research. HHS also stated that the agencies continue to evaluate the best approach to providing NIH and VA with access to DOD's medical research information.

We are sending copies of this report to the appropriate congressional committees; the Secretary of Defense, the Deputy Under Secretary of Defense for Personnel and Readiness; the Deputy Under Secretary of Defense for Acquisitions, Technology and Logistics; the Assistant Secretary of Defense for Health Affairs; the Secretaries of the Army, Navy, and Air Force and the Commandant of the Marine Corps; the Secretary of Health and Human Services; the Secretary of Veterans Affairs; and other interested parties. In addition, the report is available at no charge on the GAO website at http://www.gao.gov.

---

[20]GAO-12-342SP.

If you or your staff have any questions about this report, please contact Linda Kohn at (202) 512-7114 or kohnl@gao.gov or Brenda Farrell at (202) 512-3604 or farrellb@gao.gov. Contact Points for our Offices of Congressional Relations and Public Affairs may be found on the last page of this report. GAO staff who made key contributions to this report are listed in appendix III.

Linda T. Kohn
Director, Health Care

Brenda S. Farrell
Director, Defense Capabilities
 and Management

List of Committees

The Honorable Carl Levin
Chairman
The Honorable James Inhofe
Ranking Member
Committee on Armed Services
United States Senate

The Honorable Chairman
The Honorable Ranking Member
Subcommittee on Defense
Committee on Appropriations
United States Senate

The Honorable Howard P. "Buck" McKeon
Chairman
The Honorable Adam Smith
Ranking Member
Committee on Armed Services
House of Representatives

The Honorable C.W. "Bill" Young
Chairman
The Honorable Pete Visclosky
Ranking Member
Subcommittee on Defense
Committee on Appropriations
House of Representatives

Appendix I: Comments from the Department of Defense

THE ASSISTANT SECRETARY OF DEFENSE
1200 DEFENSE PENTAGON
WASHINGTON, DC 20301-1200

HEALTH AFFAIRS

JAN 16 2013

Ms. Linda T. Kohn
Director, Health Care
U.S. Government Accountability Office
441 G Street, N.W.
Washington, DC 20548

Dear Ms. Kohn:

This is the Department of Defense response to the Government Accountability Office (GAO) Draft Report, GAO-13-209, "DEFENSE HEALTH: Actions Needed to Help Ensure Combat Casualty Care Research Achieves Goals," dated December 19, 2012 (GAO Code 291032).

Thank you for the opportunity to review and comment on the draft report. After careful review, we concur with the report recommendations, but would like to offer technical comments. My response to the recommendations contained in the draft report is enclosed.

My points of contact for this action are Dr. Terry Rauch (Functional) and Mr. Gunther Zimmerman (Audit Liaison). Dr. Rauch may be reached at (703) 681-8390, or Terry.Rauch@ha.osd.mil. Mr. Zimmerman may be reached at (703) 681-4360, or Gunther.Zimmerman@tma.osd.mil.

Sincerely,

Jonathan Woodson, M.D.

Enclosures:
As stated

GAO Draft Report Dated December 19, 2012
GAO-13-209 (GAO CODE 291032)

"DEFENSE HEALTH: ACTIONS NEEDED TO HELP ENSURE COMBAT CASUALTY
CARE RESEARCH ACHIEVES GOALS"

DEPARTMENT OF DEFENSE COMMENTS
TO THE GAO RECOMMENDATION

RECOMMENDATION 1: The GAO recommends that the Secretary of Defense direct the Under Secretary of Defense for Personnel and Readiness to direct the Assistant Secretary of Defense for Health Affairs to issue the final Joint Program Committee 6 Charter to formally establish clear agreement on roles and responsibilities in the area of Combat Casualty Care research and development.

DoD RESPONSE: On January 2, 2013 the Joint Program Committee 6 Charter was signed and issued by the Commanding General, U.S. Army Medical Research and Materiel Command, consistent with the provisions of the Interagency Support Agreement between the Office of the Assistant Secretary of Defense for Health Affairs and the U.S. Army Medical Research and Materiel Command. Therefore, this recommendation has been completed.

RECOMMENDATION 2: The GAO recommends that the Secretary of Defense direct the Under Secretary of Defense for Acquisition, Technology, and Logistics to communicate to DOD's non-medical research organizations the importance of coordination with the Joint Program Committee 6 Chair for combat casualty care issues, and require this coordination early in the research process when these organizations conduct research with implications for combat casualty care.

DoD RESPONSE: Concur

RECOMMENDATION 3: The GAO recommends that the Secretary of Defense direct the Under Secretary of Defense for Personnel and Readiness to direct the Assistant Secretary of Defense for Health Affairs to develop and implement a plan to assess the extent to which combat casualty care research and development addresses gaps in DoD's capability to provide combat casualty care and achieves DoD's other goals for this portfolio of research.

DoD RESPONSE: The OASD(HA) Combat Casualty Care research portfolio review and analysis process evaluates the alignment of research efforts to the identified capability gaps as well as other DoD research goals on a regular basis. We will revise the current process to better assess the extent to which each Combat Casualty Care research project closes the identified capability gaps. The revised plan will be used in subsequent Combat Casualty Care research program reviews to assure that research efforts align to capability gaps, to analyze the extent of gap closure, to assess the current state of research and science, and to identify other gaps that provide additional research opportunities.

Appendix II: Comments from the Department of Health & Human Services

DEPARTMENT OF HEALTH & HUMAN SERVICES   OFFICE OF THE SECRETARY

Assistant Secretary for Legislation
Washington, DC 20201

JAN 1 5 2013

Linda T. Kohn
Director, Health Care
U.S. Government Accountability Office
441 G Street NW
Washington, DC 20548

Dear Ms. Kohn:

Attached are comments on the U.S. Government Accountability Office's (GAO) report entitled,
"DEFENSE HEALTH: Action Needed to Help Ensure Combat Casualty Care Research
Achieves Goals" (GAO-13-209).

The Department appreciates the opportunity to review this report prior to publication.

Sincerely,

Jim R. Esquea
Assistant Secretary for Legislation

Attachment

<u>**GENERAL COMMENTS OF THE DEPARTMENT OF HEALTH AND HUMAN
SERVICES (HHS) ON THE GOVERNMENT ACCOUNTABILITY OFFICE'S (GAO)
DRAFT REPORT ENTITLED, " DEFENSE HEALTH: ACTIONS NEEDED TO HELP
ENSURE COMBAT CASUALTY CARE RESEARCH ACHIEVES GOALS" (GAO-13-
209)**</u>

The Department appreciates the opportunity to review and comment on this draft report.

In this report, GAO references previously identified issues concerning the ability of the
Department of Defense (DoD), the National Institutes of Health (NIH), and the Department of
Veterans Affairs (VA) to readily access comprehensive medical research information funded by
the other agencies. GAO stated, "the three agencies could improve their ability to efficiently
identify potential duplication if they improved access to each others' comprehensive electronic
information on funded health research."

All DoD and VA research scientists and program administrators have had access to award data
on NIH-funded health research via the public database http://report.nih.gov to determine
potential duplication of NIH's and VA's funded research. Further, all NIH and VA staff and one
DoD official have access to an NIH internal database that contains comparable data on NIH and
VA grants and unfunded applications. NIH only makes the internal database available to other
federal agency officials contingent upon acceptance of a formal data access agreement.

Those data access efforts are only one part of the equation. NIH continues to evaluate with its
DoD colleagues the best approach to achieving NIH and VA access to DoD medical research
grants and applications. NIH and VA access to a DoD database of medical research grants and
applications is necessary to identify research directly related to NIH and VA programs and to
reduce the risk of potential duplication.

1

Appendix III: GAO Contacts and Staff Acknowledgments

GAO Contacts	Linda T. Kohn, (202) 512-7114 or kohnl@gao.gov Brenda S. Farrell, (202) 512-3604 or farrellb@gao.gov
Staff Acknowledgments	In addition to the contacts named above, Will Simerl, Assistant Director; Steve Boyles; La Sherri Bush; James P. Klein; Monica Perez-Nelson; Michael Pose; Mike Silver; Sarah Veale; and Cheryl Weissman made key contributions to this report.

GAO's Mission	The Government Accountability Office, the audit, evaluation, and investigative arm of Congress, exists to support Congress in meeting its constitutional responsibilities and to help improve the performance and accountability of the federal government for the American people. GAO examines the use of public funds; evaluates federal programs and policies; and provides analyses, recommendations, and other assistance to help Congress make informed oversight, policy, and funding decisions. GAO's commitment to good government is reflected in its core values of accountability, integrity, and reliability.
Obtaining Copies of GAO Reports and Testimony	The fastest and easiest way to obtain copies of GAO documents at no cost is through GAO's website (http://www.gao.gov). Each weekday afternoon, GAO posts on its website newly released reports, testimony, and correspondence. To have GAO e-mail you a list of newly posted products, go to http://www.gao.gov and select "E-mail Updates."
Order by Phone	The price of each GAO publication reflects GAO's actual cost of production and distribution and depends on the number of pages in the publication and whether the publication is printed in color or black and white. Pricing and ordering information is posted on GAO's website, http://www.gao.gov/ordering.htm. Place orders by calling (202) 512-6000, toll free (866) 801-7077, or TDD (202) 512-2537. Orders may be paid for using American Express, Discover Card, MasterCard, Visa, check, or money order. Call for additional information.
Connect with GAO	Connect with GAO on Facebook, Flickr, Twitter, and YouTube. Subscribe to our RSS Feeds or E-mail Updates. Listen to our Podcasts. Visit GAO on the web at www.gao.gov.
To Report Fraud, Waste, and Abuse in Federal Programs	Contact: Website: http://www.gao.gov/fraudnet/fraudnet.htm E-mail: fraudnet@gao.gov Automated answering system: (800) 424-5454 or (202) 512-7470
Congressional Relations	Katherine Siggerud, Managing Director, siggerudk@gao.gov, (202) 512-4400, U.S. Government Accountability Office, 441 G Street NW, Room 7125, Washington, DC 20548
Public Affairs	Chuck Young, Managing Director, youngc1@gao.gov, (202) 512-4800 U.S. Government Accountability Office, 441 G Street NW, Room 7149 Washington, DC 20548